# How to Write Internet Sales Pages That Sell

## 1. GRAB THE HEADLINES

The first basic element of an effective Internet marketing (IM) sales page is the headline. Just like a newspaper sells based on the front-page headlines, your IM sales page is going to get viewers on the basis of the main headline. Thus, you have to be sure to make this as persuasive as possible while listing in one sentence the single biggest benefit your product or service has to offer to the potential customer.

## FONT SIZE MATTERS

Whatever your headline, you want it to be written in the biggest font found anywhere on the sales page. That means that it is meant to grab attention and using the size of the font this way really sets it apart. Don't be too creative on the font type, as you want to make it very easy to read; however, be very careful to make it the biggest text on the page, as that does matter.

**USE A BIG TRIGGER**

There are numerous psychological triggers that will produce an immediate reaction with your audience. You should study these triggers, understand the demographic you are marketing to, and then choose one that is more apt to appeal to your market segment. For instance, say you are selling a product that could have many competitors in the market. So, you want to make sure that whomever lands on your sales page that they order from you, rather than taking the time to scope out the competitors and compare offers. You find that your demographic consists of business people who are used to deadlines and want to get a good deal. So, you implement a time limited offer to trigger buying behavior now and make it uncomfortable for them to take the time to look elsewhere for fear of losing out on a great deal. In that case, you list your biggest benefit, but you also make it clear that the offer is only available for the next 12 hours or until the product is sold out.

## THE THREE-HEADLINER STRATEGY

Some marketers like to make use of a three-headliner strategy. In this example, you have a pre-headline to introduce the main headline. It is not as big as the main headline and doesn't necessarily list the biggest benefit. It just sets the customer up to read the second, and main, headline. The second headline is the one with the biggest benefit and trigger. It should be a statement or offer that immediately provokes an emotional response. After that, there is a final headline that is much smaller and that gives any additional information to clarify the main headline. This approach works well and provides more space to be thorough with your main headline.

## 2. INTRODUCTION AND TYPES OF TRIGGERS

Every good news story starts with a hook, and your sales page will also want to implement this technique. A hook can be one or two sentences that really grab the imagination and attention of the reader. There is a real art to creating effective hooks, but mainly it is something that will cause the reader to pause slightly and that will trigger an emotional response. If the hook is effective, it does just what its namesake says: It hooks the reader into reading the rest of your sales page.

Let's be clear here. No one likes to spend a lot of time reading sales letters. Generally, a large number of people out there find reading to be a chore. So, you have to make it interesting and exciting. You have to get the reader to want to read the rest of the story. Without the hook, the headline isn't enough. You have to take into account the way people skim a story or sales page to decide whether it's worth reading thoroughly. First, they read the headline. If that grabs them, they will read the first few sentences. Then, they will most likely skip to the bullet points or the subheadings to decide whether to dive into the sales letter deeper. If your first few sentences are a bore, that's about the time you will lose that Web surfer to some other Internet marketer. You have to make those first few sentences count because that may be the only thing a visitor reads to decide whether to go on with your offer or not. That's why using psychological triggers to provoke a response is very, very important.

## TYPES OF TRIGGERS

As a sales person, you have to know that people buy on impulse many times. They may give you a rational explanation after the sales is completed, but ultimately, much buying behavior is an emotional response to a particular marketing trigger. Some of the triggers you can use are:

- **Ease of use**
  If you've found a solution to a problem that seriously uncomplicates people's lives, you will get a lot of sales.

- **Status**

  If your demographic is wealthy, then they may be seeking status symbols to set themselves apart from common folk.

- **Belonging**

  People join all kinds of groups where they feel a sense of community or belonging. If you can tie your product or service to some group identity that is large and lucrative, you can get quite a number of sales using this trigger.

- **Risk Aversion**

  If your customer stands to lose by not taking you up on a time limited or quantity limited offer, they will bite to close the sale more often than not.

## 3. ESTABLISH CREDIBILITY

When someone visits a sales page, they may not have any idea who you are or why they should buy from you. In order to make a case that you are indeed trustworthy, you have to either list your credentials or get other people to vouch for you. There are a number of different ways you can convince the average visitor that you are a genuine businessperson and not just some Internet scam artist. Here are a few good ways to reduce the resistance to buy from you, simply because they don't quite know who you are or whether your business is legitimate.

## FLAUNT YOUR CREDENTIALS

If you have degrees, teach seminars, written a book, or done anything that can establish a personal connection and authority on the subject you are selling, be sure to flaunt it. Nothing sells better than a person who is keenly involved in the field that they promote.

## PROVIDE TESTIMONIALS

You can write up testimonials that others provide to you. Preferably, they should include real results, not just gushing admiration. In order to give them authenticity, ask permission from the person who offers the testimonial to reprint their quote with their full name. Adding a city and state also gives it more credibility.

## POINT TO FAVORABLE REVIEWS

Did someone else give your products, service, or business a review? If it was favorable, post a link to it on your sales page so that they can see that you really are who you say you are and can provide what you say you do. If you don't want to post a link, quote the article and list the reference that gave you the review.

## GIVE OUT CONTACT INFORMATION

This seems very simple, but many IM people bypass it for fear of being "too available." You don't have to give out a physical address, but having a phone number or email address where people can reach you to ask pre-sales questions is good. It shows that you are an actual live person who is doing business online and not just some scam website.

# 4. SHOOT OUT THOSE BENEFITS!

When someone asks you why they should buy your product or service, it's a good thing to have tons of benefits ready to list. Benefits sell products, as any good marketer knows. You can't have too many benefits, so don't be afraid of listing too many. How you list those benefits is just as important as what you list.

## BULLETED LISTS

If you go through a number of Internet marketing sales pages, you'll find they almost all have one thing in common: a bulleted list of benefits. This is the best way to list your benefits because of the way people scan a sales page before deciding what to read. The bulleted list makes it easy to scan the major benefits and then read any details if the main benefit is appealing.

## ORDER IS IMPORTANT

The order of the bulleted items is important too. You want to list the biggest benefits first and work your way down. Again, this is because people tend to start to read and then lose interest the more they read. So, to keep them reading, put the juicier benefits at the top and work your way to the weakest benefits at the bottom of the list.

## WHY MORE IS BETTER

You might think that listing two whole pages of benefits is a bad idea. Actually, there is no way to list too many benefits. The reason for that is that you don't know why someone has landed on your sales page or what trigger will make someone push the "Buy" button. Since you aren't a virtual sales agent, your copy has to do the job of overcoming all objections for you. You aren't there to hear the objections running through the visitor's head. Only he/she knows what those objections are, and so the copy has to address each and every objection someone might have by listing all of the benefits the product can create in a person's life.

Eventually, as the visitor reads the list, he/she will come upon the benefit that may be the biggest trigger for him/her, but it may be placed further down the list. There's no way to know what exactly triggers that particular individual, but when he/she gets to that benefit, that may be enough to sell him/her on your product. So, be sure to list as many benefits as you can think of, even if the list runs several pages. If the visitor doesn't want to read them, he'll/she'll simply scroll onto the next subheading.

## 5. EXPLAIN YOUR FEATURES OR SPECIFICATIONS THOROUGHLY

Have you noticed that, so far, we really haven't explained much about the product or service we are selling? That's because you're not trying to sell a product or service; you are trying to sell benefits. Benefits sell products, and once the decision to buy has been made (which is typically an emotional response), then you can start to list the features or specifications of the product or service in detail.

If you were to try doing it the other way around, you would more than likely bore people to tears. Ever have the uncomfortable experience of walking into an electronics store and being assailed by a tech geek trying to sell you the latest computer based on the features and specs of the machine?

Odds are, you don't know why you'd want a certain speed of machine, why one video resolution is better than another, or what any of those weird terms the guy is spouting mean. It's just plain awkward. You aren't there to buy a particular machine based on the specs and features. You are there to buy a machine that solves your problems and makes your life easier.

If those features and specs do that, great! But no one wants to know how they work; they just want things to work. They also definitely don't want to have to guess from the features of specifications how that machine is going to work out for them. They want to be told how it solves their problems and benefits them personally. The same is true of any sales copy you write to sell products or services on the Internet. Benefits sell; product features and specifications should be detailed, but only after the benefits are listed and clearly explained.

## BE PRECISE AND HONEST

No matter what you are selling, try to give a very thorough detailing of the products and specifications. Are you selling a CD set of seminars for financial investing? Then clearly state how many CDs are in the set, how many hours of seminars they'll enjoy, and what types of exercises or teaching is involved. Don't just detail the products, though. Get them to understand how they can expect to receive the product and the timetable for delivery.

Whatever you promise in the features and specifications should be exactly what you deliver. If you want a repeat customer, don't try to con anyone into buying something that is actually less than what you've stated. Particularly in these harsh economic times where no one wants to lose money, delivering a product or service that actually exceeds the customer's expectation is the best way to retain loyal customers. That's what you want at a time when paying customers can be sparse and hard to find.

## 6. INCLUDE POWERFUL IMAGES

The Internet is the perfect medium, not just for sales copy, but also for inserting images that create that emotional reaction that is going to lead to a sale. People tend to react much more strongly to images than to words, and while people can escape from reading your copy by scanning the page, it's not possible with images. If you want to really grab the reader and make him/her want to read your copy, be sure to add some powerful images to the sales letter. Here is the correct way to do this.

## THE TOP OF YOUR SALES PAGE

Add a banner image that can really spur the imagination of your reader and get him/her excited about your copy. It's not enough to just put a logo or a bland image of your product; instead, tie it into your headline. Are you talking about how the biggest benefit of your product is that it keeps you from wasting paper? Why not show an image of someone drowning in paper and trying to find that one piece of paper they need to complete a project. Then, the headline can tie into the picture with the benefit that relates to the picture.

## SPREAD THROUGHOUT THE COPY

Add images every couple of pages or so to bring the reader through your copy as he/she scans the sales page. Be sure to put a witty subheading on the image to bring out the point you are trying to make. Keep these images much smaller than the banner image as they are meant to draw the reader further into the copy, not to hog the limelight or steal the show.

## USING TRIGGERS WITH IMAGES

Some of the ways to impact the psychology of the reader who visits your sales page is to use visual triggers. Humor is a sure way to draw the reader into your copy; just be careful not to make it crass, unprofessional, or so simplistic that it insults the reader. There's a fine line between humor and disgust.

Hitting the right note can lead to a wonderful way to connect to the reader and bring them into a more intimate relationship with your products and services. The best types of humor are the ones that take some common facet of human behavior and lightly pokes fun at it. It immediately brings in the reader who can relate to the image and helps to put them in position of being able to laugh at the human condition. It's absurd, but it can also be an opportunity to sell your biggest benefit if your products or services are able to confront that situation and provide a result.

## 7. PROMOTE VALUE OFFERS
## AND BONUSES

During tough economic times, the single biggest marketing strategy is to provide value. Consumers, these days, are seeking value like they haven't since the advent of the Great Depression. It's not enough that your product has the best features in the market; it has to be the best value too. That means that you will have to prove to the visitor who stops by your sales page that he/she is getting exceptional value for his/her money. There are several ways to do this without actually having to come out and compete on price.

## INCREASE PERCEIVED VALUE

Value is very subjective. Often, it's not price that determines value; it's the quality of the offer. That's why benefits sell. The more benefits something provides, the higher the perceived value of a product. To increase perceived value, you want to make sure that you provide much more product, or quality of product, for the price than what your competitors are willing to provide. Bonuses to the offer, especially when you use the word "free," tend to really excite customers who love getting something extra for nothing. It's also a great way to increase the perceived value of an offering.

## SOME VALUES THAT ARE IMPORTANT NOW

Also, the type of benefit is important when determining value. You won't find many people wanting to buy housing as an investment right now. However, housing as shelter is a good value in many depressed markets. How you frame the offer to get it to sell is dependent on the value that the consumer wants, not the value that your product actually has in the marketplace. So, frame your offer using some desirable values in today's marketplace: economy, frugality, longevity, quality, smart buys. Things like convenience or luxury just aren't good values to sell on right now when money is so tight that people are willing to give these features up to get better value for their money.

## PRICE IS IMPORTANT, BUT...

It's not the only thing. Don't compete on price to raise the value of your offering. This is financial suicide. If everyone competes on price, there will be very little profit to be made and you'll soon be out of business. Instead, focus on adding value through things that cost little money, but create an impression of high value, like infoproducts, higher customer service, and potential usefulness and longevity of your offerings.

## 8. MAINTAIN A SUITABLE ONLINE PRESENCE

If you are selling computers, your online presence will want to focus on an image of professionalism and efficiency. If you are selling skateboards online, the image you want is to be fun and up on the latest skating trends. You want your online persona to be authentic, and also suitable to the market niche if you are using it to sell your products or services. Not everyone wants to be known as an expert in the products and services they target, but those that do have to pay special attention to this area.

Online consumers are very savvy, and putting your name in a search engine is going to bring up everything you've got online. Don't try to play games by presenting one online image one place and another somewhere else. Be as authentic as possible and develop your credibility this way. At the very least, keep from associating with other people of dubious character or whose values contradict with those of the image you are trying to present for yourself personally or for your business.

## AUTHENTICITY COUNTS

You may have a profile on several social networking sites. If that's the case, you know that authenticity counts. You can't put up a fake name, fake interests, or fake credentials and not eventually be tripped up by it. People talk about other people, and you want to make sure that what's being said about, particularly online, is positive and beneficial to your business. The way to ensure that is to be as honest and open as you can be about who you are and what your products and services are about.

## SPONSORED OR CELEBRITY TESTIMONIALS

Some people pay for testimonials to help them achieve instant credibility in the eyes of the public. Sometimes, it is a venture partner who wants to promote your products and services for free because they benefit him too and he has more experience and credibility in the field than you. Having his or her name in a testimonial can generate sales. Other times, you get people to sponsor your products because they are a celebrity. Either way, if something happens that makes that celebrity or sponsor appear to violate the professional image you need to sell your products, you have to remove their testimonials and sever the relationship with them. Only associate with people who can promote the image you need to be consistent in the values you are promoting. Bad press for them can definitely mean bad press for you and loss of sales. Guard your professional online reputation very well by making sure the things being said online about you are positive.

# 9. ORDERING: A CALL TO ACTION

Every sales page should have a call to action. You might think that visitors have enough self-initiative to find the "Buy Now" button and click on it. Often, that's not the case. People should be led every step of the way through your sales page so that they know what's expected of them and what you can offer them in return. It may seem simplistic, but asking for the sale is one of the most important things you need in your sales page. It can literally double your effectiveness by making that call to action.

## MAKE ORDERING EASY TO SPOT

It's never too early to ask for the sale on a sales page. You want to ask for it at the very top after your headline and subheading. You want to ask for it midway through the sales page at regular intervals and you want to ask for it at the very end too. In order to make it easy to spot, you want to create buttons that graphically indicate a "clickable" spot on the page. You can do the same with a text link, but a "Buy Now" button is far more effective, both visually and logically.

## MAKE IT SIMPLE ENOUGH FOR A CHILD

You want to give really clear instructions for the ordering process. It should be as if someone who has never ordered online suddenly found your site and wanted to order. How would you explain the ordering process to them? This is the way you want to make things: Simple enough for a child to understand how to order. You should have step-by-step instructions that are very easy to follow and leave no room for misunderstanding.

## GIVE NUMEROUS PAYMENT OPTIONS

Especially during the recession, fewer and fewer people want to break out the credit cards, or they have lost their credit. Make sure you offer multiple ways to make a payment. Offer PayPal for those with online PayPal accounts.

Include directions for people who might want to pay over the phone or who want to mail in a check. If there are additional fees for International orders, be sure that you are clear on that.

People who want to buy something from another country often use PayPal, as the money can be directly converted into dollars or other denominations from their account. Offer payment plans, if that's possible, as this can be a very popular feature during tough economic times. You'll even see retail stores offering layaway, something unheard of when store credit was easier to get. Whatever way you can make it easy, offering more payment options to help the customer make the choice to buy is going to help your bottom line.

## 10.    CLOSING THE SALE

If after reading everything, or at least the important pieces of your sales page, and your visitor is still musing over the sale, you need to try one last time to close that sale. This would be in your final paragraph or two and it/they should be as convincing as you can make it. In these paragraphs, summarize the most important points of your sales letters. Try to reiterate the best benefit and hit a couple of psychological triggers that make it uncomfortable for the reader to leave the page without giving your offer a second thought. After making your final appeal, again, ask for the sale.

## SOME TECHNICAL FEATURES TO HELP

There are some technical features you can implement on your sales page that can help you close that sale. One of them is a simple pop-up screen that asks the visitor to rethink the offer before leaving. This can be annoying for some people; some people may even have pop-ups disabled on their computers. It is worth a try and can be an effective way to try to generate one last interaction with the visitor before he/she moves off of your sales page.

Another technical feature that is less intrusive is a chat window that is available to the person who still has some pre-sales inquiries. You don't necessarily have it come up when they move off your sales page, but you make sure they know that you have customer service representatives who will talk them through the offer if they still have questions. This is a very effective way to close a sale as it is much harder to say "no" to a real live person than it is to say "no" to your copy.

If you have the money to hire representatives who can close the sale, it can be a great way to generate business. It's also considered far less intrusive because the visitor makes the decision to chat by clicking the link available in the closing statement, rather than having some offensive pop-up demanding their attention when they try to leave. Some people get so offended by the pop-ups that they decide not to come back, but it's still a good way to try to catch people before they leave.

## FIND EXAMPLES AND SPLIT TEST

One of the best ways to find out how to write effective sales pages is to take a close look at the ones that inspire you to buy. Just hop online and start to do your own research by visiting your competitors' sites and seeing how they have built their pages to generate sales. There's no reason you can't use some of their strategies on your own pages. You may even discover some psychological triggers you weren't aware of, but that are very effective for your market niche. Just be sure not to copy their sales copy verbatim. That's called plagiarism.

Instead, look for the ideas behind the words and the marketing strategies they are using. Then, build your own sales pages with your own words and images to help you achieve even better results. If you're not sure what's working, you can always do a split test and set up two versions of the same offer.

Direct half of your traffic with a small piece of code on a re-direct page to one offer and the other half to the other sales page. The one sales page that creates better results is the best format. This way, you can continuously improve the design and effectiveness of your sales page by trying out different techniques. Start slowly by changing just one element of the sales page if you are doing a split test, like offering two versions with a different headline. Once you do that test and figure out which headline works best, you can move on to a split test on the call-to-action element. Slowly, you will get a better idea of what works for your demographic and products in a way that is uniquely suited to your business and product offerings.

www.ingramcontent.com/pod-product-compliance
Lightning Source LLC
Chambersburg PA
CBHW031504210526
45463CB00003B/1075